Falling Through the Madness

A book of poems by Kylie McGeehan

Edited by Devin McGeehan
and Heather Ponda

Kylie McGeehan

CONTENTS

TRIGGER WARNING: This book contains content about anxiety, depression, overall mental health issues, self harm/suicidal thoughts, rape/sexual abuse, eating disorders, alcohol abuse, and more. Please make sure you are in a good head space when approaching this book of poetry.

If needed please use the following resources:

-SAMHSA's National Helpline: 1-800-662-HELP (4357)

-Mental Health Hotline: https://mentalhealthhotline.org/ or 866-903-3787

-988 Mental Health Emergency Hotline

-Teen & Young Adult Help Line Text "Friend" to 62640; chat at nami.org/talktous; call 800-950-6264

Intro Poem

I read my own words
Words of hope
Words of hurt
Words of healing
And it feels like they came from someone else

I relate to them, I feel them in my soul
But I don't sound that dark and twisted do I?
I don't hate the world that way?

But it was all me, my very own words
Words of spite
Words of hate
Words of death
Words drip, drip, dripping with pain

ANXIETY

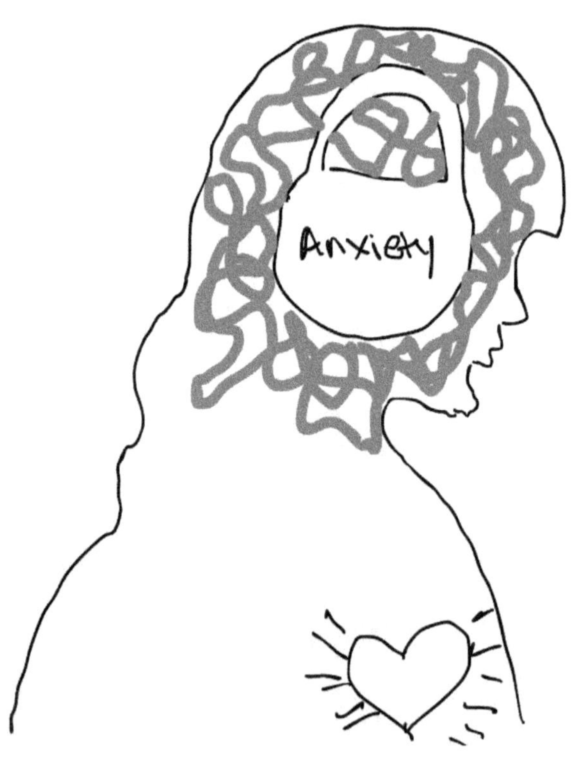

Anxiety I

They picture anxiety as this cute, put together, slightly pacing girl
And I think to myself, have I ever been that calm with anxiety?
To me anxiety is crippling, hiding under your desk at work,
Crawling into bed at 1 pm to sleep the day away because you can't
handle it,
Hiding in the closet in the dark, with your pillow and a blanket,
Blocking out extra stimulation, jerking various parts of your body
uncontrollably.
I would love to be calm and pretty when I'm anxious,
But I'm just in plain survival mode, trying to get through the day.

Anxiety II

The Anxiety crawls up my body,
Slowly sucking away the feeling that my body is my own,
Slowly sucking the life out of me.
I start to feel the pain in my chest as my lungs feel compressed,
claustrophobic, painful.
They're suffocating. I'm suffocating.
I barely notice my heart until it's about to rocket launch out of
my chest
It feels so fast and irregular. But I check and it's not.
It's 10 in the morning and this workday is seeming longer and longer
And harder to accomplish minute by minute.
I feel my sense of pride and my determination to succeed pulling
together
The thin threads of what's left of my composure.
Questions flood my head of what if's and what could be's,
What may never be and what I am willing to fight for.
I'm suffocating; help me.

I take a breath, but the air doesn't feel refreshing or relieving.

Instead, it feels like acid, burning its way through my lungs, hot and painful,

It makes my insides shrivel up, crawling decrepitly away from the one thing that should bring relief,

Yet repeatedly fails to do so.

My body stiffens, tenses, and hardens, waiting for whatever physical symptom of this disease will come next.

Because that's what this is, right?

A disease, an abnormal condition that negatively affects the structure or function of all or part of us.

Not hell. Not some form of purgatory. Not being burned alive.

It's a panic attack. Anxiety. All consuming and fierce.

Anxiety.

Anxiety IV

Why does it burn so much? The anxiety?
It burns as I breathe in, my lungs breathing in the acidic heavy air.
It burns in all the nerves of my body.
It burns as I tense and relax different body parts.
It burns in my heart, feeling like some kind of heart attack.
No amount of water calms the flames,
No amount of medicine is making this go away,
There's no extinguisher for this fire.
So I sit, and I burn.
Putting on my smiling face for all others to see.

Anxiety V

Where do I feel my anxiety? Where is it centered?
You ask from the other side of a computer screen.
"I don't know," I want to shout, "like everywhere"
But then I stop and think about what you really mean.
I feel it in my stomach, in my gut first,
It starts to clench and twist and turn like no other,
Like Silly Putty twisted to look like a Rainbow Twist Lollipop.
Then I feel it in my heart, and it starts to beat out of my chest,
Like in a cartoon when the character falls in love, except it's not cute
or romantic.
Then I feel it in my skin, the vibrations and electricity running
rampant,
Like the energy filled throughout an electric fence at all times.
Then, of course, my head spins like a madman, and I go crazy,
Going one way, then another. Hiding under rocks. Jumping out of
airplanes. Insane.
So I guess my anxiety is centered in my gut?
But then spreads like wildfire. Is that the answer you wanted to hear?
Does that suffice as an answer?
Because otherwise, I have no idea
Because by the end my whole body is out of control.

Anxiety VI

No one thing's occurred.
There is no stream of thought that I can pinpoint
So why am I having a panic attack?
What's it like to not have to experience that,
Almost every single day?
I feel like reality is not real,
It's actually some cruel existence,
That's supposed to torture me.
Painful and slow
As the breaths seem to hurt more and more
And my heart seems like it wants to end up on the floor
My panic is all-consuming
I feel so frozen in place
Like I don't know what to do
Or where to be, or even how
To even exist without some assistance

Anxiety VII

I feel like a tin can being crushed to bits
My toes feel like they might fall off from how hard I'm curling them
Trying desperately to self-comfort
And though my heart rate is normal, it feels like a spaceship
Anxiety runs through my veins, and neither the prescriptions
Nor the home remedies are helping
Why does it feel like this, what have I done wrong?
Is this some cruel punishment for something I did or said?
My muscles can't take the rapid-fire flexing that I'm doing
My brain can't find the thread of thoughts that led here
I'm scrambling; I don't know what to do.
Please save me

Anxiety VIII

Anxiety beats on the inside of my chest,
But the beating is more like pounding,
And my heart is like a racehorse,
And I sit here exhausted from doing nothing.
Nothing but internally fighting to survive,
Fighting to calm myself, fighting to be free,
Of the chains of anxiety that keep bringing me back,
To this point where I feel trapped.

Anxiety IX

My body feels like it's being strangled
As in the fear becomes a trap
The anxiety the hook
I'm a fish flopping around
Hoping for one more chance at freedom
At feeling normal
But that wish is never fulfilled
As the trap becomes tighter
Strangling my soul
And the anxiety overpowers my heart
Causing it to give out

Anxiety X

Everything makes me anxious and wary
Everything seems impossibly scary
Every tiny step seems like 10 giant ones
Every bone and muscle in my body weighs 1000 tons
The anxiety takes over, and I'm losing control
The anxiety takes over, and it's like a giant black hole
The anxiety takes over, and I'm on high alert and paranoid
The anxiety takes over, and I'm sucked into the void
Every breath I take is filled with heavy air
Every breath I take feels impaired
Every breath I take makes my heart race faster
Every breath I take reminds me anxiety is my master

Anxiety XI

It's crushing me.
The weight of the world
The weight of my thoughts
The weight of the worry
The weight of the sadness
It's crushing me.
I need some relief
I feel like the blocks in WALL-E
Compressed cubes of nothing
It's hard to breathe
It's crushing me.

Anxiety XII

I sit and watch my dogs sleep peacefully
Wishing for that same level of tranquility
But inside, everything turns and twists
Something is wrong, my body insists
But it's just anxiety
That never truly sits quietly
I feel like my heart is a racehorse
Pushing against my chest with such force
I curl up like my dog, small and in a ball
And hope that somehow it gets rid of it all

Anxiety XIII

This anxiety is different
It really hurts on the inside
I'm used to the fire that anxiety brings
The breathlessness
The burning
The panic
But this deep, deep ache
Everything hurts as I feel anxious
It's a different kind of feeling
The feeling of fear
The fear of losing you forever
The fear of never hearing your laugh
Or hearing your stories
This panic is different
It's like impending doom
That knows the feelings will worsen
Before they get better

Anxiety XIV

Tick tock
The incessant sounds of the ticking clock
Reminding us that our time is numbered
It's paralyzing and I feel encumbered
Even when the clock is quiet
My nervous system goes on a riot
Because looking at the numbers of the clock,
My head still feels the tick tock

DEPRESSION

Depression I

How can you hurt and be numb?
Cry and be strong?
Make decisions and not fall apart ?
How can it all happen so fast?
How can it change so quickly?
Or so it seems because you had blinders on
Telling you it was going to get better.

Depression II

I'm too full of the shit life has dealt to put on a smile and be social.
I'm too overcome with sadness and pain to make small talk.
I'm so close to losing it that I can't face the world and keep fighting.
Instead I just want to lie in bed under the covers, hiding.
No I don't want to get up and take the dogs for a walk.
Words are spinning in my head like a garbage disposal,
So don't be offended when I don't want to have a long conversation
Especially about your problems which seem so far away right now
And I'm so disconnected from the words you say
Just get me out of this funk and let's go on vacay

Depression III

Stuck in my body, stuck in my head.
Time spent just wishing I was in bed,
So uncomfortable to just lie here and breathe,
Looking fine but there's torment underneath.
My anxiety builds, rocketing into the sky,
My stomach turns on me and I just ask why.
Why was I put here only to feel this way?
Why are these feelings my normal?
Why is this okay?
Why is pain a thing and feelings treated abnormal?
Why? Why? Oh, Why?

Depression IV

Miserable, lying on the bathroom floor,
Please help me, God, I can't take much more.
Lying in bed, tossing and turning at night,
There has to be something I can do to make it alright.
What did I do, or who did I make so upset
To deserve all the shit that I get?
What can I do or what do I say,
Aside from carrying on and pretending it's okay?

Depression V

Your stupid alarm clock with the obnoxiously bright numbers,
Is something I consider to be a symbol of my depression.
I can't sleep because I'm anxious about being depressed,
And I sit and stare at those numbers glowing in my face.
I lie in bed trying to sleep so I don't do anything else,
And those numbers glow vividly in my face.

Depression VI

These chains draped around my neck,
And the stilts that I walk on,
Lift me up and weigh me down.
My internal dialogue:
Should I be happy, Don't be happy?
Should I be happy, don't be happy?
Should I be happy, don't be happy?
Should I be happy, don't be happy?
These chains bind me, make me feel obligated,
Keep me from being free.
The stilts are like a fake happiness that teeters this way and that.
Should I be happy? I know I can't. Not like this.

Depression VII

Thoughts flood my mind, to my depression; their calling,
With a constant drip, drip, drip,
Of the same obsession again and again.
My mind and mood are falling,
From steadily trip, trip, tripping,
Over the stumbling thoughts so,
Deep into the abyss I go.
Buried under the thoughts like accumulating snow,
My insides are rip, rip, ripping,
Apart, in piles of shredded anguish,
Until it's black and I'm numb,
If you have happiness, please share some.

Depression VIII

Empty bottles.
Depression and anxiety are empty bottles.
Empty prescription bottles that are constantly needing refilled,
Never quite making things better but making them manageable,
Empty bottles of energy and motivation that never fill,
Empty bottles of emotions that can't be felt yet are overstimulating,
Just surrounded by empty bottles.

Depression IX

Have you ever just stood there standing in the mirror
Unable to recognize the person staring back?
As tears stream down your face and you tremble in fear,
Everything around you becomes black,
And you just realize that you have no clue
Exactly how you ended up here with so much wrong,
And feeling so down and blue?
Somehow your life has become a tragic song,
That people sing along to but don't truly know
What the words really mean or how if feels.
Eventually the tune may change though
If the person standing in mirror ever truly heals.
But at that moment, the person staring back at you,
Doesn't seem like someone who can heal,
And you wonder what it is that you can do,
To flip the switch on the way you feel.

Depression X

I feel it crawling, claws reaching out
"It's coming back," I want to shout
The depression is taking over once again
And if it overtakes me, what happens then?
The sleep that is never enough,
Because being awake is just too tough.
The sadness or the numbness, not sure which I prefer,
Everything around me becomes a giant blur.
I thought I would be fine,
Or that the phrase "on the mend" could be mine,
But once again, I'm feeling pulled under.
How many more times until I sunder,
And there's nothing left,
And only those who truly know me will be bereft?

Depression XI

I sit, and I stew in my feelings and my pain
And I want to scream out loud and release this agony
But when I go to scream, nothing comes out
It's silent, not even a whisper or whimper
Everything is stuck inside, trapping me
I'm stuck in these emotions, in this pain
And no one will ever know
Because all around me is silence
And all I can produce is silence

Depression XII

They say to see the world through rose-colored glasses
But depression is the opposite of rose-colored glasses
The opposite of electronic glasses for the color blind
Instead of a cheery, rosy tint to the world
You see the world all gray and bleak
Instead of seeing new colors
You see what exists in black and white
The world keeps spinning, and time passes
Things continue on, and you fall behind
And all the attachment to others you've had becomes frayed and curled
What once was strength now seems weak
A pain so powerful and acidic it's sure to give you ulcers
And it seems like nothing can make the world seem right
But hey, look at the world through rose-colored glasses

Depression XIII

There's a level of sadness, that is normal to feel.
But then there's sadness where you need help to heal.
You lie in bed staring at the wall,
Wishing you could shrink away from it all.
Where every organ in your body is hurting,
And words fail you, and negative thoughts are inserting,
"I wish I was dead," "I can't do this anymore."
It goes on and on as you stand behind your internal door,
Trying to shut everything out,
That's the sadness I'm talking about.

MENTAL HEALTH

Mental Health I

I tell myself that it's going to be okay,
Like it's not the millionth time today.
Trying to reassure myself of my strength
But did someone change the day's length?
Because it seems a lot longer
Everything takes me being a lot stronger
Mustering up a polite voice and a deceiving plan
Trying to cover up the fact that I don't think I can
Don't think I can keep breathing
Don't think that my heart can keep beating
Don't think I can keep feeling this way, anymore.

Mental Health II

How is it that some people have it all easy?
Like that rich white girl whose biggest struggle
Is that her nail broke, and she can't get it fixed today?
And barely has to work to get the spot we've all been dreaming of
Since only like forever.

Or the white male whose parents coddled him
Whose biggest problem was trying not to cheat too soon.
Who still lives at home not a single bill to pay,
Who gets whatever he wants regardless of consequences.

Then there are those like me who are beaten down time and time again by society.
Told that they're not normal, not meant to fit in, not enough
Who tries so hard and still falls short because the challenges they face overcome their dreams and ambitions.
Those like me who spent so long trying to fit in the cookie-cutter shape of society,
Who no longer try to fit that mold and still fall short when they reach for the stars.

Some people have it all easy.
Like that white man sitting on the hill telling women what to do with their bodies,
Or that committee member who looks at my application and says it's not enough,
Then there are those like me.

Mental Health III

I mute my phone and lay in the cold, quiet, dark room.
Exhausted from this new journey on which I've chosen to embark,
Which may have been worth nothing, which I'm beginning to see.
And the family drama that's never-ending is taking its toll on me,
I worry about my grandpa, alone now that my grandma has passed away,
I worry about my brother, who is losing his way,
I worry about my sister, struggling to enjoy stuff,
I worry about my other sister, who I don't talk to enough,
I worry about my mother, who's caught up in some drama,
But I push it all down, trying to avoid more trauma.
But it never really goes away, does it?

Mental Health IV

Alone.
Isolated and alone.
Surrounded by people and still alone.
No one knows how I feel,
And I'm told not to share.
I'm unable to talk; my lips are sealed,
No one around me cares.
No one wants to hear the negativity,
That comes out of my mouth.
I'm alone.
I feel like I'm on an iceberg,
Destined to sink,
Because I just feel so alone.

Mental Health V

Some days, food stresses me to the max,
Some days I say fuck it and eat like this meal's my last.
I try to be healthy, but that sugar calls my name,
I try to be healthy but really my control is to blame,
For the terrible relationship that I have with food
For the way a change of meal plans can put me in a mood.
I need to control the numbers, control what I take in,
The calories, the fat, the carbs are all a sin.
Food should be enjoyed and healthy and fun
But I don't know that the eating disorder way of thinking will ever
be done.
I look at the scale each morning as the numbers change
They're like a rollercoaster that has free-range
Up and down and up some more
Man, it's a big step onto that scale from the floor
I hate it, but I need it
So complicated, and the way I pick an outfit
Is based on what the numbers say, and what I need to hide
The numbers on the scale take me for a wild ride.

Mental Health VI

Why am I so tired? Why do I shake so much?
Oh yeah, it's the medications leaving a lasting touch
Side effects, on side effects, on side effects, and more
Leaving you feeling like you'll never make it out the door
But these feelings are different than before
Will they put you on more medicine to sweep the side effects away
Or take away the medications that get you through the day (barely)
Why am I so tired? Why is everything a chore?
What does feeling normal even mean anymore?

Mental Health VII

I'm suffocating, choking on my own thoughts.
They twist and turn around me forming a network of branches
That traps me within.
They join together and build nets that entangle me,
Wrapping around my throat.
The thoughts overpower everything and take control
And I'm left suffocating, throat closing.

Mental Health VIII

You know I want you
Or at least want to want you
But my body won't respond
It's stuck in the trauma
Stuck in the hurt
And it freezes up
And I'm left feeling like dirt
Or somewhere lower than that
Because you deserve
Everything you desire
I just wish my internal fire
Had more umph to it
More fuel to feel good
But I don't
Sometimes not even a bit
And I'm fucking tired of this shit
I want to do what I want
I want to be what I want
But that trauma still paralyzes me
Please someone tell me
How to be free

Mental Health IX

How is that these 4 walls
Can seem like a trap
And a safe haven at the same time?
I feel stuck in one place
Like the walls are shrinking in
And there's not enough space
And I'm isolated from the world.
But is being isolated good or bad?
I feel comfortable here,
Going out makes me anxious.
I'm scared that they'll get me
"Who's they?" you may ask
Honestly, I don't know
"Get me how?" Don't know that either
I just know that my safe place,
On days like today is my cage as well.

Mental Health X

In front of a group of people I stand,
Smiling like I have it all together,
Talking like I know all the answers.
Sometimes I want to shout "I can't do this",
And run out.
But then I think of the need for the money
And the passion for knowledge
I think of my resume and what this could mean
So I smile and I talk.
Talk.
Talk.
Talk.
Until I drag my feet home
And crawl into bed
Because trying to keep it together
Messes with my head.

Mental Health XI

I'm at work, but I really don't want to be,
I'd rather be at home under my blankie.
Not like I'd truly sleep for real,
I haven't done that in over a week but still,
There it's easier to pretend like the rest of the world doesn't exist.
There I can be numb, my emotions don't resist,
I can pretend like there's no cancer, or suffering, or pain,
Like there's no secrets clawing at my brain,
Like misery and pain just float away,
Because I am safe and okay.

I call you not because I need your voicemail over and over.
Or your loss for words, she's crazy, stunned silence.
That just confirms the fact that I'm crazy.
I don't need you to mumble out the words I'm here for you,
Like a robot or a disk on repeat.
I need you physically here for me,
Holding my hand,
Telling me I can do this when you can actually see what I'm going through.
I call you not because I need you home in an hour or two,
Or because time is going to fix what's going on,
I need you to be here, to hold me, to see me struggle,
I need help, oh God, I need help.

Mental Health XIII

Who did I piss off to have this bad luck?
If one thing good comes along,
It's followed by 20 bad things,
Car problems,
Back and other health problems,
Debt upon debt,
Medication changes,
It just never ends.
It makes it hard to justify
The reason to move on
To keep going and not end it.
Bad luck, upon bad luck

Mental Health XIV

I sob on the phone but you don't care
I silently beg you to come home
But you don't understand my pain
I know that this isn't fair
Me interrupting your workflow
But you're the only sure comfort I know
You say you have to go back to work
My heart rips into pieces
Please help me each tear screams
As I put the phone down

Mental Health XV

Maybe I should be happy for or proud of myself
I've made it to 27, and I'm still kicking
Even though there were times I wanted to die
And there were moments I thought I'd never get through
I've made it to this point; I can make it farther
But it doesn't always feel like that
And that's okay as long as I keep pushing on
And ask for help when it's needed.
Maybe I should be happy for and proud of myself
But I'm just not and I don't know why

Mental Health XVI

I feel like I'm wading through water
And with each step, it gets deeper
My thoughts splash over me like violent waves
My actions replay in my head like sinking sand under my toes
My pain takes me further and further under the water
Soon, I will be drowning
The thoughts and actions flowing over my head
My breath unable to function
My muscles unable to push me to the surface
Just stuck underwater, drowning

I know in my bones that coming off this medicine is the right thing to do,
But the process of doing it has made me so blue.
I sit in bed wishing for sleep to overcome the feelings I feel,
Wishing I didn't need so much medication to truly heal.
There's the argument that it's all a trauma response and no medicine will really do the trick,
And maybe that's partly true, but I think it's also a chemical imbalance making me sick.
I'm trying to be able to function at work and not shake
But how many weeks of med changes will that take?
And how many of those weeks of feeling not okay,
Can I wither and face each and every day?

Mental Health XVIII

I think of the long list of things I need to do
And the unhappy feelings begin to brew
And begin to shrink and shrivel up into myself
Happiness haphazardly tossed on the shelf
Overwhelmed, anxious, depressed, and more
Are now what I'm feeling because my facade tore
The heavyweights bringing me down
The anxiety makes me worry and frown
The depression like a big black hole
And all the feelings together are taking their toll
I need to reset, to sleep, some pills
Something, anything, as my mind fills
With negativity and heaviness
Someone, please bring back my happiness

Mental Health XIX

How is it possible to be so lonely, when you're surrounded by people?
But I guess I've done it to myself in a way
I'm not outgoing, I don't gossip, it's hard to have fun
I've put up walls with no windows
And I'm not about to take them down
But sometimes the loneliness creeps up
And overwhelms everything in me
And the world seems so big and empty

Mental Health XX

Write it down, scream it out
Open your mouth and silently shout
Draw it and put it on display for all to see
Just don't keep it bottled inside, trust me
It'll eat you away like moths and old fabric
You'll get labeled as psychotic
It'll crush your soul, you'll lose your hope
You need some way to cope
Have I found the right way, the perfect answer
Hell no, no way, not me, no sir
But I'm trying not to bundle it inside anymore
Trying not to have to be picked up off the floor
But it's a work in progress, a growing trait
Now, if only I could keep my head on straight

4

SELF HARM

TRIGGER WARNING

Please note- I am not promoting self-harm or suicide. I am merely sharing my experience with suicidal ideations and self-harm. If you are feeling suicidal please reach out and text or call 988.

Self Harm I

They take away your go-to right?
For me, it's the pills
The very ones that are supposed to help
Yet haven't been lately
They take those away and then feel safe abandoning you
But they don't realize how many other options you have
For instance that robe tie in the closet
Makes a pretty surefire way to hang yourself
Or those knives in the kitchen all lined up in a drawer
It's like playing eeny meeny miny moe, picking which one to use
To make a cut, or two, or three
At least one so deep blood pours out from me
Those chemicals under the sink sure won't taste great
But with no one left to call for help, they'll poison me
Ending this terrible state
They take one away, then feeling safe, leave you alone
But they don't realize how dangerous these thoughts can be

Self Harm II

I say I'm overwhelmed
They say aww we all get that way sometimes too
And I say no I don't think you understand
I have hundreds of thousands of things
Pushing on the inside of my skin, trying to get out
I feel ready to explode, or implode or something big
But nothing happens and I feel an urge
An urge to cut, to give an escape route for those things stuck inside
An urge to shrink up in the corner of my closet
To shrivel up and die
I need some escape, and I'm desperate
I feel more than others feel
More intensely than most people feel
And I just need some relief
I'm overwhelmed

Self Harm III

I don't deserve to be here, not anymore
Taking up people's time and taking up space
I'm doing my best to keep upright and not crumple to the floor
But I don't belong here; this is no longer the right place
I just keep making costly mistakes
Like an idiot who cannot manage to do any better
How much longer until my body and soul breaks
Maybe it's time that this body spreads her wings and flies

Self Harm IV

I'm bleeding out
Blood gushing and dripping and more
And still, I find no relief from the pain I feel
The pressure of the world that shoves me down
It still sits on my shoulders, hunching them forward
Weighing me down till I feel lower than the ground
Enough for me to drown, drown in my own misery
Now I'm drowning, stuck in the pain
And still, there's no relief for things I've seen
The panic makes my lungs unable to expand
The pressure in my chest feels like a ticking time bomb
It's enough to squeeze an elephant and shred them to pieces
Do you ever sometimes wish that you were dead?
Because right now, I do
Now I'm lying awake, wishing that I'd die
The hurt, the anguish, the pressure
It's all too much for me, too much to bear
And I look towards heaven, wishing I was there

Self Harm V

"I want to die" I think to myself
"I don't want to be here anymore"
Yet I don't have a plan
Don't intend to take any action
Just like, I'd be cool, you know
If I could just maybe not wake up tomorrow
It it could just all be over and done
The panic, the pain, the emptiness
It would be over and I'd finally be at peace

Self Harm VI

I get pierced, I get tattooed
I get blood drawn, I get a shot
And guess what; I like it, I enjoy the pain
I feel free when that sharp needle pierces my skin
When that stinging sensation takes over
I feel relaxed, I feel calm, I like the hurt
What the hell is wrong with me?
What is screwed up in my head?
Why does the hurt set my soul on fire
Set it free into the sky
Why do I find comfort in the pain?
Because the external pain I can control
I can choose when and where, how and why
But the internal pain doesn't work that way
I can't control it, it controls me
It stabs and it aches, it twitches and shakes
I hurt inside my heart, I hurt inside my soul
I hurt in my own mind, I hurt everywhere

Self Harm VII

I feel the pain sear through my body
And then put a Band-Aid on
Hoping that it will be noticed by nobody
But the pain isn't gone
I can still feel the raw ache of reality
Of what I have just done
Some may describe what I did as brutality
But I just describe it as for a moment the emotions won

Self Harm VIII

The familiar sensation of self destruction begins
My mind is imploding, there's no way to win
I feel the drag and pull of the idea of nothingness
Pull me under as I process less and less
"End it" the enchanting voice inside my head calls
I try not to think of the pills over there by the wall
Or the knife that would be so easy to find
My mind is fighting but it's in a bind
To live, or to die
But how much more can I try
How many more self destructions can my head take
What words said against me will take the cake
And push me over that final edge, oh it seems so nice
But it would indeed be a big sacrifice

5

CHRONIC CONDITIONS

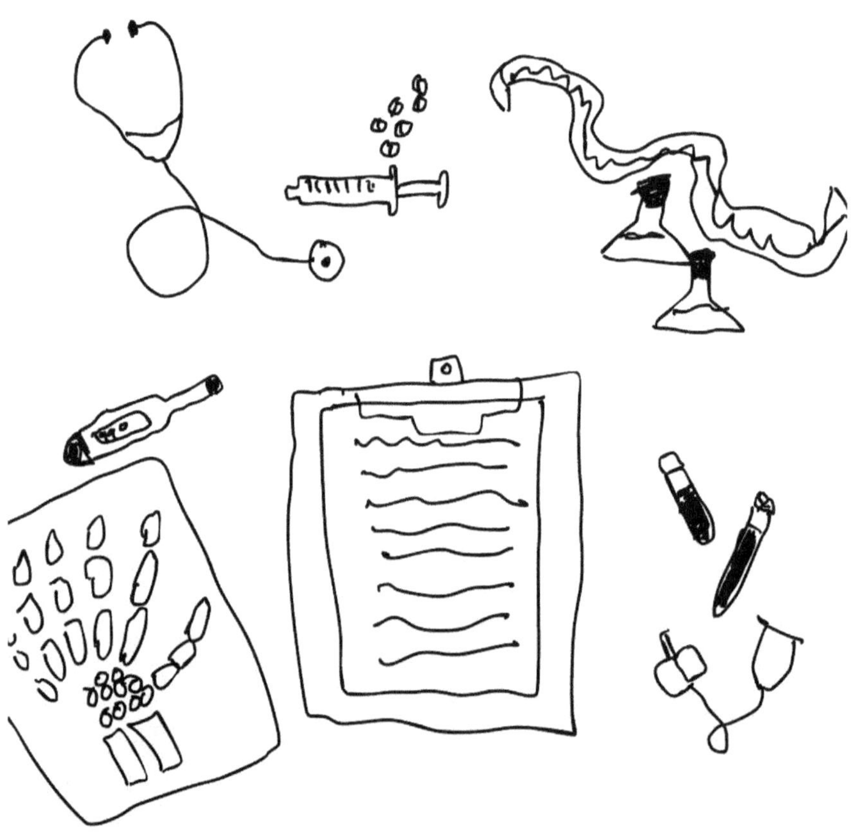

Chronic Conditions I

They don't listen to me.
They're laser-focused on my long list of medications,
While I silently beg for help
But they sit back flabbergasted by all the complications.
It's how I function, all the medications (at least for
now),
It's how I get up each morning and put one foot in front of the other,
And at least, usually, I don't malfunction.
Lately, it's been getting harder, and I wish for something other
Then they want to "detox" me of my lifelines
Or hospitalize me and take away what I enjoy.
But I can't, not now, even as my health declines
Now I just need help for the anxiety that's starting to destroy
Everything I care about
So please just listen
Because without any doubt
I know more about my condition
So zero in on me, the person, and forget about the rest
Please focus on me and my words, because I know me best

Chronic Conditions II

Please don't abandon me here on the kitchen floor
When I'm begging for help
Don't leave me like this, in this state of vulnerability
Like so many others have done in my past.
Please don't leave me here, hiding in the closet
When I need you.
In these moments, I don't need you to save me
I need you to help me save myself and fight on.
Please don't go
Don't choose a job over me.
In sickness and in health, remember?
Unfortunately, you have to see more of the former, and I'm sorry
Please stay with me
Hold my hand
Kiss my forehead
Tell me bad jokes
Just please don't abandon me here
On the unwelcoming floor, becoming smaller and smaller.

Chronic Conditions III

The world spins around me like a tilt a whirl and I can't tell if I'm grounded or not

The bile in my stomach is churning and throwing up is taking everything I've got

I sleep as much as I can but I'm dehydrated and need medicine

I call for help but my voice sounds like shaking gelatin

But the help I get doesn't help and they recommend the hospital

But the hospital doesn't help either,

and I just want to go home after a week AMA

So I say I'm okay and that everything's fine

And I sit and I struggle to to have everything in line

But the world still spins and I'm still in pain, all of my asking for help was in vain.

Chronic Conditions IV

It hurts to do anything,
Anything and everything.
Pain that won't go away with ibuprofen,
Or even the prescriptions they gave me.
So I sit here, not moving,
Not living my life,
Wasting away on this chair.
Sitting and pretending the pain
Just doesn't exist,
Oh, wouldn't that be nice?
But it does
And I feel it
Oh so strong
Taking away the enjoyment
Of doing anything

Chronic Conditions V

They say they want to help
But help would be listening and not analyzing every word
Finding new ways to do things,
Instead of shoving the other ways I've already tried down my throat.
Help would be letting me vent without lecturing,
Respecting my beliefs and not trying to force theirs.
Help would be physically being there for me when I need them,
Doctors, friends, loved ones
They all say they want to help
But maybe I'm just going to be stuck being unhelpable

Chronic Conditions VI

"Oh how can I help?"
I know that's supposed to be constructive
And helpful
But instead, it's suffocating.
Because if I knew,
Don't you think I would've fucking told you?
If I had a life sucks magic 8 ball
With all the answers to what would help
Don't you think I would vocalize it?
I do want help
But I don't know the answer to that question
I don't know the answer to a lot of questions
But especially that one
Because if I knew we wouldn't be here
So stop asking if you can help and start actually helping
Jump right in, do things that have worked in the past
Things that you would want if you were in my shoes
It doesn't matter, but don't just stare at me asking, "How can I help?"

Chronic Conditions VII

Crackle, pop, snap
There goes my neck and my back
As I get cracked like a glow stick
This chiropractor better help my migraines
I'm so desperate for relief
So desperate to not miss any more work
So desperate to not go back to the hospital
So desperate to better
So, with another crackle, pop, and snap
I sit up, dazed and confused
As I'm sent on my way

Chronic Conditions VIII

Crying like a baby in the doctor's office, feeling ashamed
I just want answers, and to no longer be in pain
I want a fix for my problem, for the agony to be named
But the longer this goes on, the more I think it's all in my brain
And then what? How do I fix how fucked up my head is?
I cause my own problems that cause even more issues
"I'm sorry" and "I wish I could fix it" is what everyone says
But I'd love for them to live a day in my shoes
I'd love for them to live without answers or solutions
I'd love for them to live like me

Chronic Conditions IX

Is this really my life?
This rollercoaster of emotions,
Anxiety, depression, PTSD,
This constant pain,
Migraines and fibromyalgia,
Is this really my life?
Or even a life?
How do I feel good?
Besides the medications?
How do I form relationships?
Is this really my life?

Chronic Conditions X

I feel lost, stuck, shoved down to a certain kind of hell
But despite this, there's still part of me that wants to be well
To see the future, see the good
See the changes that only time could bring
To see me be healthy
To see my marriage last
To see myself as a mom
To see us be a little more wealthy
To see the disappearance of demons of my past
To see me surrounded by family
To see me old and wrinkly, going on about stories from the past
I may feel lost, stuck, and shoved down
But I want to keep moving on
To see the future and the good it brings

Chronic Conditions XI

I can't eat, I can't drink, I can't sleep, I just lie still and cry

My stomach hurts like hell, but no one can tell me why

Is it all in my head, am I going crazy, inventing problems that don't exist?

Or is there just something they haven't found yet, or something they missed?

I writhe in pain like demons are trapped in my abdomen

Maybe I should take all the vomiting and nausea as some kind of omen.

I just want to cry because I can't take it anymore

Another thing that leaves me curled up on the floor.

My head hurts. I want to scream.
I'm not as okay as it may seem.
The full agony of my head feeling like it's shrinking,
While my brain is going, "what are you thinking?"
The pressure behind my eyes is undeniable,
If I just lived in the dark and quiet would that be viable?
The band, the pills, the nose spray,
None of it helps, at least not for long anyway.

Chronic Conditions XIII

The pain starts in my lumbar spine
Radiating up and down
And the muscles around it tense
My back is screaming
And inside, so am I
I tried to work through the pain
But it just got worse and worse
Now I'm letting people down
I'm screwing us over with money
I'm not at training for my new job
At what point do you accept it
That you have to take care of yourself
And at what point do you fight
And get through things, suffering through
I'm worried they might fire me
I'm worried they might not give me a chance
I need to transfer trainers
Maybe they'll do that sooner?
But for now I have to take care of the pain

Chronic Conditions XIV

You "fix" me with pills and therapy
But it's like taking a jagged gaping wound
And taping the edges together with scotch tape
We try and we try to keep it closed
Or in other words, to keep my composure
But inside, the infection is spreading
While the numbness allows me
To placate everyone's expectations
But you are "fixing" me
Can't keep the wound closed
I'm just too broken and injured

Chronic Conditions XV

So much to do and so little time
Just kidding, my body is just in pain
This stage of life is definitely not my prime
Problems seem to fall on me like rain
It's true there's so much to do
But the problem isn't time for me
I try to pick one thing, or maybe a few
But sometimes even that's not even meant to be
As I lay here wishing I could feel normal
But what does that even mean
Everything I do is sloppy and informal
I need to try out a better routine

Pain.
Pain.
Pain, pain, pain, pain
It all come back to pain
Physical pain that feels like your breaking
Emotional pain that makes you feel less than whole
Why can't you leave me alone?
Why can't I just be free for good?
There's only so much someone can take before they break
And I'm on the verge.
Nothing gets rid of the pain once it starts
It's consuming me, becoming my identity.
Pain.
It all comes back to pain.

Chronic Conditions XVII

They say I'll get better but I've given up on asking when
I juggle my different appointments but sometimes I feel forgotten
Or unseen, unheard,
Under prioritized, under valued
Like even when I listen and follow every word
It's never enough to be better
Is it on me or is it on them?
Is my destiny to struggle through every day?
I dream of feeling better but that version of better is beginning to fade
To disfigure. To disappear.
Because I don't know when it may come.

Chronic Conditions XVIII

I don't feel good today
But how is that anything new
"Everything hurts" I say
But the meaning swerves around you
I slept the day away
Another day wasted it seems
I wish health and happiness were here to stay
But that's only possible in my dreams.
When I say "everything hurts"
It's usually mentally
And physically
Emotionally too
But again the meaning soars past you
Saying everything hurts
Literally means everything hurts
So I sleep to keep the pain at bay
I sleep and waste another day away

Chronic Conditions XIX

The pain violently explodes from every neuron firing in my brain

As I lie in bed and try not to move, which at this point, my body is trained for

I breathe in and out, every so carefully, so that the pain doesn't worsen

But also so the nausea doesn't turn into actual vomiting

The pills, they don't work

So, as I so luckily have the time for right now, I pray for sleep to take over

I sleep deep but awaken with no relief and I wonder when will the pain end

Chronic Conditions XX

I writhe in pain and scream in agony
Waiting for your comfort anxiously
But all you do is stand there and look
A response so cold, my whole body shook
The pain is excruciating, someone please help me
Make the pain go away, help me I plea
I'm curled up on the bathroom floor
While my cries echo from door to door
You do nothing to help or comfort me
So I'm left to drown in my discomfort

6

RELATIONSHIPS

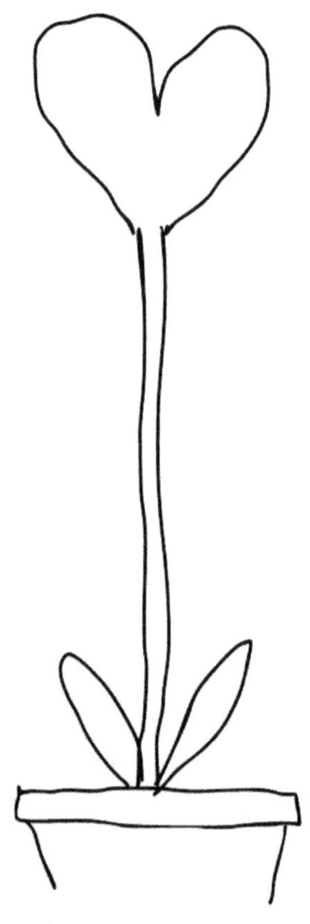

Relationships I

You. It's you
All along, I've been ashamed
Thinking it was me
But it's you, it's always been you
Don't throw my medical bills in my face
For the pills that I need just to maintain
Some semblance of normalcy inside my brain
For the literally keeping me alive or something like that
It has no comparison to us always compensating for your stupidity
And your dumb ass choices when you don't listen to reason
Or listen to me
We have constantly had to bring you back from your gaping black
holes
That are caused by the messes you've made
Or the time when we had 9,000 and you brought us down to 6
Without a single word to me or a plan to quit
It is you that has us scrambling for finances with your high insurance
And your car collecting dust in the garage
Or the wide variety of bills piling in our mailbox
It's you, it's always been you
So don't throw it back in my face
Don't you dare even think about it
That's been done to me all my life
I won't stand for it happening anymore

Does the concept of divorce of your parents
Become easier at any age?
I've been through it as a young kid,
Now, as an almost 30-year adult
My siblings are 17 and 18.
Does that separation ever get easier?
Does it ever hurt less or feel less like your fault?
Does it ever make you question love less?
Does it ever make you contemplate your choices differently?
Does it ever feel less like a stab to the heart?

Relationships III

I watch as she is attacked, blamed, and shamed
Until she feels so small, she accepts the hate
I watch as she is manipulated and controlled because
Well, he has money, and she doesn't
I watch as she becomes so unhappy I feel her anguish
I want to be able to set my mom free from her chains
But I don't know how

I watch as she is lectured for being who she is
Given grief and attacked for dressing how she feels
I watch as she applies for colleges out of country, just to get away
from him
I watch as she grows stronger in her beliefs to defy him
I want to help my sister feel empowered and want to stay close
But with him around, I don't know how

I watch as he struggles, a relationship with both sides
They have a movie night/sleep on the couch tradition that they've
continued on
I watch as he argues his beliefs and believes so differently than his dad
But he can't let go, can't say anything bad, can't hurt his dad
I want to help my brother see the manipulation without taking
away the love
But I don't know how

Relationships IV

Is it jealousy, normal sibling rivalry, or shared trauma?
What is it that fuels the sibling unease in my veins?
I'm proud of her, sure
Love her? Of course
But when we are together, it's like a competition
Where one of us has to one-up the other
Or outshine them somehow
It makes me uneasy and anxious
I'm not going for hatred, but my blood boils nonetheless
It's uneasy, it's uncomfortable, it's not like with my half-siblings
It's seeds of doubt of how the other really feels
Or is it our relationships with our father that differ extremely?
And wounds that never really truly healed

Relationships V

Oh, you ghosted me, what a shocker that is.
Yet it makes me sad because once upon a time
I would have thought we'd have been there
For those big moments in each others' lives
Like finding the right man, the right dress, saying I do.

But now, just meeting for coffee scares each of us away.
How did this happen? What am I forgetting?
I remember you choosing them over me.
What is it that I have done? What is it that I had said?
That you kicked me out of your life?
Turned me away like unwanted trash?
But then, why did I reach out, thinking it would be different this time
Thinking you might still care.

Relationships VI

I had friends, once upon a time
So what happened to those "friends"
Maybe it's that I drove them away,
With my excessive worry and need for validation
I was too clingy and weirdly depressed
I was someone who was fun in a group but not on her own
I drove them away with my own madness
Maybe, just maybe, that's what happened

Or maybe time changed us, turning us into the people we are now
We started liking different things; we moved to different places
We found faith or lack thereof
We fell in love and traveled the world, and our eyes opened to
different things
I'd like to think this is what happened and that I didn't drive them
all away
But I still grieve the loss of them as I am solitary now

Relationships VII

I don't know what to say or do to make this better
Wish I had some speech written out to the letter
I want us to be okay, I really do,
But the question is do you?
I'm hurt and disappointed.
I'm out of whack, my heart feels disjointed
But I can't forgive and forget what you did
You acted like a dumbass kid
You scared me, endangered yourself
So my heart has put up a wall to protect itself
I have to figure out how to lower it
But you've got to figure out your issues

Relationships VIII

I hate my own father, I wish he was dead
I'd personally put a price on his head
He abandoned me when I needed him most
Right when I was diagnosed
Haven't spoken a word to him since
So thinking of my sister's wedding makes me wince
I'll have to put on my fake smile
Say hello and try to not throw up bile
I'm nervous and scared
I don't think I'll ever quite be prepared
To see his face for hours
As much as I try, forgiveness isn't one of my superpowers

Relationships IX

We're a slave to our phones as a society
We're a slave to social media
We're a slave to the idea of a perfect person
That is sold to us by corporations
We try so hard to be that person that we forget to be ourselves
Even work involves our phones now
And we're stuck thinking to ourselves
Put down the damn phone
Pay attention to me
See the hurt and the pain and the emptiness I feel
From the comparisons I make and the insignificance, I feel
Pay attention to me
I'm more important than that business call
I'm more important than that text, that video, than that feed
But you're a slave to your phone; I know I am, too
The both of us needing to focus more on the here and the now

Relationships X

Sometimes it's like I'm screaming at a blank wall
And my words just aren't getting through
Why don't you listen to me at all
Or are you listening and not hearing
What is it that is stopping you?
Is it that you don't care,
Or is your mind somewhere else completely
Do we need to separate and get some air
Or are you just saying "screw you" discretely
It's like I'm screaming at a blank wall
No responses or acknowledgement back from you
All my words seem to do is fall
And I don't know what else I can do

Relationships XI

I love being a big sister, it's great
It's like watching these squishy little faces
Turn into individuals and people
With hopes and dreams
With talent, emotion, and intelligence
They turn into people better than you
And better than you ever dreamed they could be
And that's the best part of it for me

I love being a big sister, it's great
Even when they get moody or ghost your text for days
Watching them grow both physically and mentally,
Even when you're stuck being the shortest somehow.
They turn into people with weird likes and obsessions
They travel the country and the world as their wings spread wide
And you just get to look at them with pride
That's another best part of it for me

I love being a big sister, it's great
I really could go on and on
But I love my siblings to death
And I hope they love me, too
And that we stay close forever
Now, that would be the best lifelong part for me

Relationships XII

I'm scared to not be okay now
I'm scared not to be strong enough
After everything we've gone through
I owe it to you
But it's so hard when I need you here
Whispering calming things in my ear
But I know I'm why you're depressed
Why you drink too much? You're obsessed
And you turn it into thinking you did wrong
Or thinking that you have to fix me
I don't need fixing; I need comfort
If it's too much, I need to know
But I also need it to be okay for me to not be okay
To not be strong enough

Relationships XIII

Your lack of action and lack of words
Speaks louder than any words could
You don't want to try
Or try to apologize
You simply don't care about me
I used to to try so hard to be your idea of perfect
I didn't complain (at least not much) when there was no food
I let you drink a 6 pack and brought you one after the other
I did good in school, tried hard at sports
Pretended like I wanted to be at your house more
You were the adult; I was the kid
Yet I spent more time taking care of you
Then you spent listening to what I needed
But now I'd rather die and go to hell
Than try to be your idea of perfect
I'd rather the silence than the lies
Even though with the lies, you tried something
I'd rather live an eternity in a fire-fueled existence
Than be what I used to try so hard to be for you
Here are my last words to you,
And they aren't much
To you, I'd say
FUCK YOU
And be done

Relationships XIV

Here's a poem to my ex
You're a liar and a cheater
Too bad you were such a weeper
Always saying you didn't know what to do with your life
Well obviously, you haven't even made her your wife
I wish you a life filled with disappointment
And failure and unemployment
I don't wish you well, as you can obviously tell
I hate you to your core
I wish I didn't have to see you anymore
For the way I was treated
Never getting the closure that I needed
Thrown away like trash when I was true gold
And you were the black persistent mold

Relationships XV

Have sex, be good
Do the things that all women should
But I can't. I freeze, my mind goes crazy
Thinking of something from my past that's still kind of hazy
I lock up tight, shut down completely
Why did someone ever hurt me
I want to do what all women should
I want to please my partner like someone else would
But I'm stuck in my trauma
Fighting all the drama and tears
Fighting through all my fears
Have sex, be good
God, I wish I could

7

GRIEF/LOSS

Mourning someone who hasn't died is such a strange thing
Were you ever who I thought or was I just naive?
And somehow we are still tied together through some weathered out string
In this situation do I celebrate or grieve
Or is this a somewhere in between sort of situation
Where I'm hanging by a thread twisted in space
Ugh my brain and heart just need some sort of vacation
I'm grieving the image of your old face
The one that actually cared and stood up for those he loved
Didn't hide behind the bottle and throw words around like knives
But now you make others feel like you, unloved
You ruined yourself, so now you come after our lives
I mourn the you, you used to be
Why is it so hard to move on and be happy?

Grief/Loss II

How is it that the ornery little lady, with a height under 5 feet,
Is also the happiest, most genuine person that you'd ever had the pleasure to meet.
A love for God, family, and Jelly probably in that order,
Led a life full of laughter so hard it led to tears for everyone around her.
Today I celebrate you and the life that you lead
It's been 3 years, a fact that I just can't absorb in my head
I miss you, great grandma, that's a fact I can't deny
But I hope that somewhere with your angel wings, you're soaring in the sky

Grief/Loss III

Today is the day that you left this earth
That you officially became an angel
Although I suspect you were one long before
I know your magical, heavenly rebirth
Was quite magical. Though losing you was painful
I never could have imagined the pain I'd be in for
But I try to remember you're still around
Watching and guiding us each and every day
Telling us you love us the mostest
I can still hear that, that laughing sound
As you enjoyed your life to the fullest
I miss you, great grandma, every day
I've realized how much that pain never goes away
But it's replaced by a fondness for the memories
A great desire to share your stories,
Though no one will ever be able to tell them quite like you.
I see you in my dreams, and I know you're here
Comforting me when I'm filled with fear.

***This is dedicated to my angel of a great grandma, Ruby Pearl Whipple who passed away in 2019 but is no doubt still looking over us.

Grief/Loss IV

Last night was my birthday celebration dinner with family (our tradition)
But there were some very important people missing, unfortunately
Cancer seems to have instantaneously taken things
It's taken the life out of my grandma, who's usually the life of the party as her laughter rings.
And the carefree feelings of my grandpa, with his bad jokes galore
And the ability for any of us to talk about anything else that came before
I felt happy before the dinner but depressed after
I really did miss her glorious laughter
I wish we could go back to before so I could cherish it more
Can I blow out my candles one by one?
There's so many things that I'd wish for
My grandma's health
My own health
Everyone's happiness
I just want more memories to cherish before that can't happen

Grief/Loss V

Every time is like a forever goodbye
The unknown looming over our heads
Each time I see you, you look less like the you I know
You hold my hand, or your frail body hugs me
And I'm afraid to let go and never get to again
Slowly, I see your mind and spirit die
My heart is tearing apart at the threads
But seeing you slowly decline and go
Is a torture that would break anyone, I guarantee
But when I get the news, what happens then?

Grief/Loss VI

Today was the day when I realized,
What swallowing back the tears really meant.
It was also the first day you didn't ask to hold my hand,
Or ask me to come sit next to you.
I wish I could say that I was surprised,
I wish that the chemo pills were making a dent,
Other than making you suffer in ways that weren't planned.
I feel like I've already lost you.

Grief/Loss VII

I'm losing me, losing you, and truly losing her too
I can work to get me back
I can work to get you back
But for her, there's no back
Cancer and chemo have ravaged her body
And I want more time, but I don't want more suffering
But how do I say goodbye
How do I lose another grandparent that I'm close to
I'm terrified, scared, selfishly thinking of myself and what I want
Another Christmas with her
Another chance to hold her hand
Another hug
I'm not ready for it to be over, not ready to say goodbye
Why does the world do this?

Grief/Loss VIII

Lungs, Liver, Kidneys, Brain, Heart
So quickly, your body is failing and falling apart
You ask if you are dying
And unlike the others who are lying
I won't say no like I know I should
I say, "If you feel like you're ready to go, you could
You don't have to be strong for us."
Even though it breaks my fucking heart
Because I feel like someone needs to say that part

Grief/Loss IX

The heart stops beating
The lungs stop breathing
And the body starts to stop
Sadness explodes around you, ready to pop
And the answer of where you go, to me is a given,
You float up, and you're in heaven
My heart is heavy, I can't even cry
Tell me why I can't even cry
I miss you already, and the pain is immense
Losing someone you love is intense

Grief/Loss X

You're gone, you're really gone
How does it not seem real
We prepared for this
We knew it was coming
And yet the hurt still feels strong
And I'm walking about my day like a ghost
Trying to hold it together
But I don't know if I can
Oh I already miss you the most
This healing is going to hurt
It already does
How do we go on without you?
I guess we figure it out

Grief/Loss XI

I feel a gaping hole in my heart
A hole that will never be filled again
That will be plastered over by cheap labor
Or even worse, have some plastic put up around it
But it will never be filled without you
You're gone, forever, and I can't seem to grasp it
It hurts like hell, and I can't seem to mask it
My heart can never be whole again
Because you left a gaping hole

SAD

I feel sad that you're suffering,
Sad that you're sick
I feel sad that my whole world is spinning,
Sad trying to imagine how you must feel

ANGRY

I feel angry at the world for making you suffer again
Angry that the doctors didn't listen before
I feel angry that my mind is struggling so hard
Angry because part of me feels sorry for myself,
and I should be focused on you

SCARED

I feel scared that I might lose you,
Scared that this might win
I feel scared that you are going to fade before my eyes
Scared that this will be the worst time of our lives.

Grief/Loss XIII

For a moment I think of you, and I feel bliss
At the idea that I will see you soon
But then I remember that you're gone,
And somehow, I'm expected to keep moving on
I physically feel my stomach bottom out,
It falls deep, not graceful, more like a crash
And my heart begins to squeeze
Like someone is trying to turn it into ash
The sadness takes its emotional toll
And now the physical and emotional mix
I have to somehow put this feeling aside,
Come up with some magic fix
But what I end up doing is just pushing it back down
So that the next time
I'll be stuck with the same emotions
And difficult hills to climb
In order to pull myself together
And look like this is a storm I can weather

Grief/Loss XIV

Life goes on, yet grief still remains
The memories with you still burned in our brains
I hope that when I talk to you, you still hear my words
As you're soaring through heaven with wings bigger than a bird's
I hope you know just how loved you still are
And that you're always close somehow, never truly far
The loss of you left a hole in my heart
And sometimes, the pain from it still tears me apart

8

RANDOM

Random I

I'm not the perfect angel I wanted the world to see me be
Or that my great grandma wishes were me
I cut, I cuss, I count the minutes until I can crawl in bed
Some days I live life to the most, the others I'm filled with dread
Some days I'm scared to walk out that door or to set foot on the ground
My anxiety tells me something bad will happen, and in my head, it goes round
Some days I'm curled up in the closet, and internally I'm screaming for someone else
My depression has a hold of me, and I can feel it, or I can turn to ice
I wanted to make my grandma proud, a woman who loved her life
I don't walk like her, I'm not happy like her, but I'm always genuinely me
Is that enough to make her proud? Just to be
I hope so cuz man she lit up a room and made everyone happy
Even though she was ornery and snappy
But she loved her life so much and had a gentle giving touch
Gosh I think about her and I miss her so much
To make her proud has always been my goal,
but when I look inside, I just see a big empty hole

Random II

Walking into work afraid I'm going to lose my job

Walking into work worried that I'm being talked about behind my back

Walking around work seeing things that tear you apart inside

Walking to the car like you can't get there fast enough

Walking into the house like fresh clothes and a face wash will fix everything

Walking toward the bed because in reality, sleep is the only escape

Random III

You think you are surrounded by a strong support system
People who love you and are willing to help when in need
Until you actually need help
And you're sticking your shaking hand out
And bobbing in the deep, icy water, alone, with no one around
Everyone fled away on lifeboats, saving themselves first
Not stopping for a minute to think of your dreams, plans, and hopes
They just leave you hanging by a thread,
Wondering whether you'd be better off dead

Random IV

I just want to cry
And watch Disney movies
And eat pasta
And wear an electric blanket
And eat a cupcake or Crumble cookie
Is that too much to ask for?
I need to break a little bit inside
So that I can heal back up
And somehow move past this

Random V

I'm trying not to sweat the losses of the past
I don't want to relive the rejection, the hurt.
But people can't even bother to say two words
Or let me down nicely with words that placate my hopeful soul.
But there's a reason that they're losses of the past
And not continuing problem starters of my current life

Random VI

Everyone has a place a job that they do
Every job is important in its own way, too
So why do I stare at that person and think
Why don't you want to be more
Why don't you want to do more
Why don't you want to make something of yourself
Become something greater
But then I think, "What is wrong with me?"
Is it the pressure of society to conform
To be a doctor to be a lawyer, to be a high-level exec
Or is it my own personal perfectionist self
Misplacing the blame onto someone else
My own unhappiness being projected
On to this poor other person?

Random VII

"It's okay."
I feel like I say that a lot
To be kind and not cause problems
Even when it's not okay
Like "I'm sorry you're in pain"
"It's okay."
"I'm sorry I broke your thing"
"It's okay."
I'm sorry you're struggling
"It's okay."
But really, it's not
It's almost never okay

Random VIII

I feel so angry at the world
For pushing all my buttons
I feel so angry at myself
For having so many buttons to be pushed
I feel so angry at life
For making me go through this
I feel so angry
I don't wanna do it

Random IX

Who gave you permission to still take up space in my mind
To go on giving me anxiety by making me feel less than worthy
It may have been almost 10 years but even your name makes me retract into myself
You cheated on me, took away "family", took away my sense of self, my understanding of love
You made everyone question my stability from a single statement
You chose her, a downgrade and a half, yet it still hurt like hell
Looking back, I know we would have never worked so that's not what hurts
You wanted to ride a motorcycle and grow a beard, I hated both
You are still living at home, and I wanted to get out, be responsible, and on my own
It would have never worked but that doesn't negate the pain that you instilled
Because the poison that you injected into my heart
To hate myself and to hate you doesn't just dissipate
If I never saw you again, it would be one thing, but I have to keep being reminded
Reminded of how disgusting you are, of how much of a waste of time it was,
Reminded that I now question the validity of what I felt, of the things I said
Reminded of you drinking your parent's alcohol and finding ways to sneak around
I remember you sitting on the left side of the bed, me at the computer,
I remember you sobbing because you didn't know what to do or who to be
Maybe a firefighter, you thought, or something in theater,
I at least never guessed what you would turn out to be was a cheater
Get out of my head, and stop taking up space and time, it's a waste

Leave me alone, like I want to forget that you existed

Get out of my head; stop putting me down

Get out of my head; you don't have permission to make me hate myself anymore

I stare at the screen, or more like through it
As I wait for the clickity-clack of my fingers as they soar across the keys
Because I've found something to write about or something magnificent to say
But every time I come close, I freeze
I'm having a rough day
The pain level is high
My focus level is not okay
And I feel so nauseous I just want to cry
There, I've said it; is that enough?
I feel like this far out from the injury, I should be doing more stuff
But I just am not ready

Random XI

I was abused as a child and a teen
I'm a survivor, not a victim
My dad and stepdad were alcoholics
I'm a survivor, not a victim
I was sexually abused
I'm a survivor, not a victim
I was emotionally abused
I'm a survivor, not a victim
I've been cheated on
I'm a survivor, not a victim
I've been abandoned
I'm a survivor, not a victim
I had an eating disorder
And I'm a survivor
I have treatment-resistant major depression with psychosis
And I'm a survivor
I have generalized anxiety disorder
And I'm a survivor
I have fibromyalgia
And I'm a survivor
I have Chronic Migraines
And I'm a survivor
Every day, I'm surviving
Maybe not always thriving
But surviving
And keeping on fighting
For the me that I want to be
Not the me; the people of my past thought I'd be
Or the me conditions of my present have tried to shape me into
I'm a survivor, and I will fight
Until I am who I'm meant to be

Random XII

Sometimes, I look at myself and panic
"I look too much like him," I think
Not wanting to resemble him at all
Not wanting to bear his qualities that were satanic
So I stand by the mirror behind the sink
My mood begins to quickly fall
I see the shape of his face
His butt chin in mine
I wonder if I act like him
My pulse quickens, starting to race
Trying my best to draw a line
Between us but, the outlook is grim

Random XIII

Sometimes I worry, that I'm doomed for the same destiny as my parents
    As my grandparents and even my great-grandparents
    The word itself sends anxiety to my soul
    NO, it screams back
    I won't be like them or end up like that
    Though DIVORCE does seem to run in the family
    But I love my husband, and he loves me, so don't you see it could never be
    Quite like that for me and him, us together
    We're stronger, healthier, happier
    We'll make it, you'll see

Random XIV

Are we indeed fictional characters in someone else's story?
Not a story about somebody else but a story in which we aren't
the author
We don't choose what happens to us; it just happens to us
Or our life is so structured, and we think we are making the choice
When we are actually being controlled and manipulated into doing
A thing that somebody else wants us to do.
I read a book today, and that was what the whole first chapter
was about
And since then my mind has been blown and stuck on a Ferris wheel
Of what ifs, and if thens, and why does the person writing my story
hate me so much

Random XV

I take a sip of alcohol, and I'm afraid
Afraid I've become like the two of you
Using the buzz to numb the pain
Using the drunken forgetfulness to hide the ugly things that my
mind wants to think about
Using the drink to not think
To not feel, to escape it all
I take a sip of alcohol, and I'm afraid
Afraid I'll end up like them
Afraid I'm broken and in pain
But the release from my own mind feels so nice
And the warm fuzzy feeling is so welcoming
But I refuse to be like them
I refuse to cope this way
To hide behind the bottle
To use it to fuel hatred and loneliness
I take a sip, and I am no longer afraid
I won't do it, won't end up like them
It won't happen, it just won't

Random XVI

Abuse
It comes in many forms
Physical
Sexual
Financial
Emotional
Elder
Domestic
Child

It comes in many forms but is never okay.
Why do we still let this happen, how is there not more help
The victims and survivors have such little voice, such little power
They're afraid, they're being controlled, they don't have the help
they need
Abuse comes in many forms, and we can stop it
But we have to want to try

Random XVII

I'll burn in hell before some old white man sitting on the hill
Tells me what I can and cannot do with my own body
We are not in the 1800s still you cannot take away my will
You cannot tell people who to love, or how to love
You cannot force me and my baby to die
You cannot arm the masses to kill the children innocently sitting
in school
You're privileged little life may not have prepared you for this
But we are strong, and you will see
We will fight and vote and come together as one
You will see we won't go down quietly

Random XIX

You ask what I'm thinking
I reply nothing but you don't believe me
But it's true; I'm just staring and blinking
Trying to not feel and just be
But the actual truth is that I'm blocking everything out
Trying to keep from feeling
The pressure and nervousness that I'm pushing about
Are fighting me back, there's an inner battle
So my head is overwhelmed by emotions, as always
But I push them down deep so I don't seem rattled

Random XX

I finally get to work in medicine with kids
But then why do I feel so many butterflies
Fluttering in my stomach as I close my eyes
The excitement train comes to a stop and skids
Scared I'll make a mistake
My heart begins to ache
Scared I won't be good
Scared I'll be misunderstood
Scared that I fucked up by taking this leap
Scared that my negative thoughts will steep
And turn into actions that'll make me weep
Scared that it'll be ruined by my mood
Scared that I turned down other opportunities, and now I'm screwed
Scared that I won't be at my best
Now the anxiety is building in my chest
My heart flutters, stuttering along
Trying to keep up and stay strong
STOP I scream to myself; calm down
How does it go? I think with a frown
I think I can, I think I can, I think I can
I mutter to myself as I make a plan
A plan to be open, to learn new things
Learn to step out and spread my wings
Take care of that child
Learn to keep my thoughts from running wild

Random XXI

The slow crawling opening door painfully gives way
As I wonder if this will be a sign of my day
Long and dragging, full of hard work, and that makes you want to go home and pop the cork
Or the type that makes you question why you went into this line of work
The ones that have you wishing and praying for some sort of change
Or one where all you want to do is return home to a nice bed you can arrange

Random XXII

They don't get it; this is my dream
They don't get it, changing it isn't as easy as it may seem
They don't get it; it's not just about the money
They don't get it, I'm not some dummy
Who takes this responsibility lightly
Who asks this favor knowing my debt is unsightly
Whose pride doesn't shatter at the seams asking for help
Who doesn't sit there crying saying, "There goes another one, oh well"
They just don't get it, don't get who I am

Random XXIII

Some small dick congressman up on the hill
Who grew up in white privilege and as a dominant male
Is trying to tell me what to do with my female body?
To that, I say hell no!
If one of your side pieces got pregnant
Abortion would look pretty good then, wouldn't it
If one of your daughters would die without an abortion
Abortion would look pretty good then, wouldn't it
It's my body, my choice
Abortion may not be for me, but I, too, grew up in white privilege
I have a husband to support me and a job to provide
But what I do with my body is not for you to decide
When you have to wear that mask for 10 minutes to keep others safe
It's your body, your choice
So how come when it's growing a baby inside for 9 months
It's not my body my choice
I'm tired of being controlled, tired of being told what to do
I'm tired of being looked at differently because I'm female
I'm tired of the catcalls and the aggressive glances
I'm tired of having to act like a lady and be so perfect
I'm tired of it not being my body, my choice

Random XXIV

People who don't watch Disney
May not see, the characters the way they come across to me
Belle is a beauty, and yet she looks like I do
Not the blue-eyed blondes with the perfect hairdo
She is stubborn and stands her ground
And by the end love and freedom she's found
Not because of some prince or some muscle man
But because of herself, because she's a woman that can
Rapunzel may be trapped up in a tower
But she doesn't sit in the corner and cower
She makes a plan
Uses a frying pan
And realizes she's the lost princess
Even though her life has been a mess
Luisa may not be petite and perfectly beautiful
But her strength is beyond powerful
She stays mentally strong to protect her family
Not just physically strong to help her community
Merida is a wild-haired wonder
Who scrambles to fix her own blunder
Her relationship with her mother grows
And by the end, she truly knows
Who she is, and what is her fate
And without ever relying on a date
Moana is also a wild spirit that calls to me
She longs to help her people and longs for the sea
She gets a demigod to put back the heart
And restores the freedom of her people who had been torn apart
That's why I chose them to put on my sleeve
That's what Disney characters mean to me

Random XXV

Give me constructive criticism
Throw me to the wolves
Let me fumble through things
I'm working to better myself
But it's hard when you're talking to everyone else
In Spanish, around me
And lecturing me about the small things
And always second-guessing me
And double-checking me
I feel like I'm behind
I feel like I'm failing
Giving me something good
Give me something positive
Training is completely draining
Especially with you as the trainer

Random XXVI

I'm trying to study; I swear I am
But my mind is off in some wonderland
That is free of pain and sadness
That is free of the pressure and the impending madness
That comes from the pills that fill my hand
I'm trying to focus. I really am
But my brain is worrying about the things I cannot control
About what people are saying behind their backs about me
About what dangerous things are out there
About every possible scenario that could go wrong
Either way, they both are the same
My mind and body want to be free
So I sit here trying to study
But instead, I'm looking at a life
That will never be

Random XXVII

Do you ever get the feeling like there's got to be something else?
Something better, something more?
Than this day-to-day shuffle of putting one foot in front of the other
And plastering on a smile and cheery voice
Something that's new, incredible, and amazing?
Something that you don't want to escape from?
Or is that just me?

Random XXVIII

I don't know how to pray
I feel like that's such a stupid thing to say
But I don't know which words to string into a sentence
Or if I need to do some type of repentance
I just want there to be something or one that I believe in
Wish I could jump on the religion bandwagon
But God has never answered my prayers
When I needed him most he was never there
So I don't know how to pray
Otherwise, I'd be doing it every day

Random XXIX

It's my body and my choice, and I'm not afraid to say
But it doesn't make the whispers behind my back go away
Something as simple as tattoos
Is some big headline creating news
Never mind that I change my hair
Or don't wear makeup when I go somewhere
I can hear your "whispers" as I pass by
But they don't bother me because you know why
It's my body; I'll do with it what I want, and please
So take it in, and let your objections float away with the breeze

Random XXX

Rape.
Rape is Rape
Just because I was coerced into consenting
I don't want this, It hurts, he's unrelenting
I shouldn't have to feel this way
I should get a say because
Rape is Rape
There's no thinking of it differently
Or changing the definition
Just because you've been coerced and conditioned
Into doing this act and having sex when it's unwanted
To feel pressured and confronted
Just because we're women doesn't make this okay
It's not part of being a woman, as I've heard people say
Rape is Rape
It's Rape

9

NOT AS DEPRESSING

You know those rare occasions when you actually feel okay
Where the weight of the world isn't on your shoulders
You're not focused on everything that could go wrong
You feel light, free, revitalized
Why are those moments so few and far between
Why is it so hard to feel that way
I went to a concert that I really enjoyed
And I felt light and happy, and you could almost say ecstatic
But I'd look over, and you'd look angry or upset
Why was my joy then brought down by my worry?
Worry about what you were thinking and feeling?
Worry for being the cause?
On that rare occasion, I had a sliver of weightlessness
That then came plummeting down.
But man, to feel that again, I would do so many things

Not as Depressing II

(written in 2022, that's crazy!)

2 years we've been married
Geez the time has flown by,
Yet it hasn't,
We've been through so much.
8 years, we've been together
Man that makes me feel old
Yet we were just babies when we met
Dreams and freedom in our eyes
No love, commitment, and devotion.
Yet that's what we found,
And together, we've grown
We've been through some of
The highest highs and the lowest lows.
Discovering new things together,
Seeing the world.
Those 8 years as yours,
Those 2 years as your wife,
Have made me a better person.
Thank you, and I love you

Not as Depressing III

2023 was like a giant roller coaster
With ups and downs and very sharp corners
My love and I traveled across the sea
Saw the Greek islands and Italy
My grandma lost her fight to cancer
We are all left wondering why- but there's no answer
Happiness and sadness ebbed and flowed
New sides of people definitely showed
A year unlike any other
Now it's time for yet another

To me, the cherry blossom tree represents resilience, rebirth, and renewal
Plus, when they blossom, they really are quite beautiful
They represent resilience - bending but never breaking
Harnessing inner strength to help come back from something that was heart-aching
They represent rebirth- starting anew or being revived again
As Buddhism says allowing one to better cultivate compassion and kindness towards all women/men
They represent renewal - to remind us to revel in our own passing time on earth with joy and passion
Enjoy the little things in life like laughter, good smells, or a stranger's compassion
Such a simple thing: a flower on a tree
But its beautiful blossom has such symbolism to more than just me

Why Disney? So many ask as the tattoos build along my arm
Isn't that a bit childish, a bit young for you, they may say
But why not Disney? I think to myself
It has been there for me when others failed to do so
It has taught me and many others things like
"You've got a friend in me"- to find your kindred spirits and hold on to them tight
It has taught me that music and "whistling while you work" makes things better
Even though I still wish woodland creatures would clean for me
It has taught us that, truly getting to know people, you'll discover things beyond appearances
Because the people who could truly learn to love a "beast" are those who look beyond your brave face
It has taught me that cast iron skillets are pretty badass, and so is sticking up for yourself
When you know in your heart that something is wrong, fight for what's right
It has taught me that even those with the biggest muscles to get through life have pressure they face, that can make things heavy
It has taught me that a woman doesn't need a man to save her; she's perfectly capable of doing it herself,
Although having one there for support is nice too,
It has taught me that love is powerful
And that friendship is magic
And that following your dreams is important
And that feeling like I don't belong isn't just a me thing
And to "just keep swimming" when life gets tough
Disney has taught me so much, that people around me failed to pass along
So why not Disney?

Not as Depressing VI

Why does being a kind human being seem to be so hard
Like, can't we do the "white person wave and smile"
(you know where you like half smile
And you bend your elbow to put your hand up shyly)
And have it not be creepy or weird
Just be kind to people
Especially those around you
Be kind; don't judge someone because they have
A different outward appearance than you
Be kind, don't judge someone because they might not
Have the money to do all the things you do
Be kind, if someone is hurting and they let you in
Be a resource of support, a kindred spirit

Not as Depressing VII

I care too much, yet I don't care at all
You people think you can make me fall
But I refuse to, I will stand tall
I may have scratches, scrapes, and bruises
But in the end, it won't be me who loses
I am a person who chooses
Each day to continue on when the going gets tough
Even when enough is enough
I may have it harder than you
But because of that, I know it's true
That I will rise each time I stumble
And you can never make me crumble
I will rise again, and I will win
So take a moment and let that sink in

Not as Depressing VIII

Cardboard box in the middle of the living room
A hard-working lemonade stand is in bloom
Inside, two young girls giggle away
As their grandparents come by to say
"One lemonade, please."
The fake lemons the girls squeeze
The glass of "lemonade" is handed out
Happiness and good times are about
Memories are made of the highest grade
and when it's important, will never fade

Not as Depressing IX

I feel the heat of the sunshine across my face
The change of seasons, I happily embrace
The bloom of the trees and the flowers
The sound of rain instead of snow showers
The sunshine fills me up with gratitude
It gives me a whole new attitude
One that is optimistic and happy
The seasons have changed, and I'm feeling quite sappy

Not as Depressing X

Grandma,
I just wanted to let you know
That you mean the world to me.
Only a heart as true as yours
Would give to others so unselfishly.
For all the things you've done
All the times you've been there
It helped me learn what healthy love looks like.
And I've never doubted how much you really care.
Even if it was not always said
I appreciated everything you did
I think about it all the time in my head
About how much I really love and respect you

**This is dedicated to my Grandmother Rebecca Ponda, who sadly passed away in 2023 due to a long-fought battle with Metastatic Breast Cancer.

Happiness
Such a simple idea but so hard to find
Especially in day-to-day life, working the grind.

Happiness
It's the sound of the ocean waves crashing on the sand
While in the background, there's the beat of some techno band
The feeling of the sun warming up your skin
The feel of the water as you finally go in.

Happiness
The feeling of a full belly, filled with delicious food
Paired with some wine that's sweet and tastes good
The feeling of good company and nowhere to be
The feeling that your soul is being set free.

Happiness
The warmth of your hand intertwined with mine
The feeling that whatever comes up, we will be fine
No interruptions or distractions or people wanting to fight
Just good conversation and company all day and night.

Happiness
Wandering the streets with no specific destination in mind
Welcoming people with smiles, that are so kind
Experiencing a culture that's different from my own
Learning new things that I've never known.

Happiness
No feelings of depression or anxiety, no pain
Except from all the walking and the distance we gain
No headaches, no jitters, no fear of the worst

It's like a totally different person just waiting to burst.

10

About the Author

About The Author:
Kylie McGeehan

Kylie McGeehan has a background in
Biomedical Science and Medicine. She is a
Colorado Native is an avid reader,
photographer, traveler, and Disney fanatic,
and loves hiking with her husband
and two dogs. She is the oldest of 4
siblings and family is very important to
her. This is her first published work.